BODY PARTS

BODY PARTS

Brian McCabe

CANONGATE

First published in Great Britain in 1999 by
Canongate Books Ltd,
14 High Street, Edinburgh EH1 1TE

10   9   8   7   6   5   4   3   2   1

The publishers gratefully acknowledge subsidy from
the Scottish Arts Council towards the publication
of this volume

British Library Cataloguing-in-Publication Data
A catalogue record for this book is available
on request from the British Library

ISBN 0 86241 877 1

Typeset by Antony Gray
Printed and bound in Great Britain by
The Cromwell Press, Trowbridge, Wiltshire

FOR SOPHIE AND CLEO

CONTENTS

LOW LIFE
Worm   3
Slug   4
Mussel   5
Ant   6
Spider   7
Cockroach   8
Eel   9
Viceroy   10
Lizard   11
Tortoise   12
Buzzard   13
Seagull   14

THE SAVAGE OBJECT
Object   17
Turnip   18
Jar   19
Kite   21
Dumpling   22
Spot   23
Floor   24
Settee   25
Coal   26
Rat   27
Stone   29
Ball   31
Objet Perdu   32

OTHER LIFE
Other Life   35
Ordinary Words   36

Sick Kid   37
Nursery School   38
Angel   39
It   41
Buddha   42
Visiting Speaker   43
Island Girl   44
Aphrodite   45
Roy Orbison   46
Surasundari   47
Reclining Nude   49
Swan   50
The Rat Catcher   51
Recruit   56
Thousand   58
Mercy   60

BODY PARTS
We   63
Scapula   64
Tongue   66
Eyelids   67
Hand   68
Feet   69
Mouth   70
Small Intestine   71
Head   73
Head 2   74
Donor   75
Skull   76
Cock   77
Ear   78
Node   79
Skin   80
Thigh   81

ACKNOWLEDGEMENTS

Acknowledgements and thanks are due to the editors and producers of the following publications and programmes:

After the Watergaw (Scottish Cultural Press 1998); Alter; Carapace (1998, South Africa); Comparative Criticism 19 (Cambridge University Press 1997); Deliberately Thirsty (Argyll Publishing 1998); The Edinburgh Review 95 (Spring 1996); The End of a Régime (Aberdeen University Press 1991); Full Strength Angels (ASLS 1996); The Glasgow Herald; The Glory Signs (ASLS 1998); The Ice Horses (Scottish Cultural Press 1996); Kaleidoscope (BBC Radio 4); Lines Review 136 (1996); The Malahat Review; Mica (1994); Northlight; Norman MacCaig: A Celebration (Chapman / BBC Radio Scotland, 1995); Not Donald MacDonald (Highland Printmakers 1996); Panta (Bompiani 1999); Poetry Wales (1991); Rebel Inc 2 (1992); The Red Wheelbarrow (University of St Andrews 1998); The Scotsman; Scotland on Sunday; A Scottish Feast (Argyll Publishing 1996).

'Seagulls' was published as one of a series of postcards for National Poetry Day 1997 by Book Trust Scotland.

The author would like to thank the Scottish Arts Council for a writer's bursary which helped him to complete this book.

BODY PARTS

LOW LIFE

WORM

I am a living thing. I curl
from the arsehole of the world

to be your prototype: begin
with the fingerprint frets on my skin;

end with the naked question mark
of my clever flesh.

Who are you, blind creature?
What is your purpose on this earth?

Stamp on me. I'm working-class.
My mates will banquet on your carcass.

SLUG

Don't you fancy me in my black
figure-hugging bodystocking
skin?

Watch me arch my agile back,
show my underside's pale line —
like an inky, questing tongue.

Do I disgust you?
I am not the only libido
to ooze from this dark earth.

Haven't we met somewhere
before? What are you doing here
on this rainy afternoon, alone?

My tapering finger is beckoning
you to your likeness.
Come on.

MUSSEL

Hello God, this is me
in my long blue burberry
with the shiny lining
sitting on my dorsal hinge
with my wee black bible
clasped tight in my shell
praying I'll no be noticed
by anybody bigger than me.
It would be good to travel
in the ballast water
of a transatlantic liner.
And to develop stripes.
A cousin of mine did that.
In the meanwhile I'll cling
to this rock of ages — or is it
just ages of rock? — anyway
please God, if you're there
— and I mean, even if you're not —
give me a grain of sand
and I'll turn it into a pearl.
At least let me procreate.

Mytilus, modiolus, mytildae.
Anodanta, unio, unionidae.

Amen.

ANT

— How long have we been marching
since the bivouac?

—Three million nine hundred and
ninety-nine thousand, nine hundred
and ninety-nine years.
Why?

— Not four? You flabber my gaster.
How many of us are left?

—We're in the upper trillions,
and diversifying all the time.

— Not the quads yet? No wonder
my variable mandibles are twitchy.

—Want to regurgitate your crop?
I could do with an oral exchange of food.
And to follow, some olfactory chit-chat,
a bit of gustatory debate.

— All you think about is your social stomach.
What about secreting a trail?
Wait a minute. My elbowed antennae
tell me something is happening —

— Mine too: the queen has shed her wings
and is sequestered in her cavity.
It's time to form a new colony.
Pass it on.

SPIDER

In a previous life, they say
I hanged myself
for winning a spinning contest
with Athene.

Lies.
In my mythology
there are no goddesses:
just me and my mate and my prey.

He'll do that dance again
with his eightsome-reeling legs
and secrete a sticky compliment
on the dark design of my web.

It's just an air-strainer, I'll say.

He'll look into my two rows of eyes
finger my silk with his pedipalps
and call me his Athene.
I'll clear my throat.

Arachne, I'll say.

To save time, I'll turn round
and advertise my abdomen.
He'll realise why he was born.
Then I'll eat him.

Sluiced in my juice,
he'll make a nutritious soup.
I may not be a goddess, but
I've still got my legs.

COCKROACH

So look at it this way.
We share the same building.
So you let us know you're coming.
We make ourselves scarce.

We don't care if it's an apartment
overlooking Central Park
or an apartment overlooked
by the census.

We care about your garbage.
True the rich have more
than the poor — but they keep it
locked up, like their art.

We have our own culture.
In one of our modern fables
a cockroach wakes up to find
he has changed into a *man*.

We're out of here. We scatter
like the coffee beans you drop
when you see us, but faster.
So we disgust you. Suits us.

We can live on your disgust.
We are spreading north.
Soon we hope to inherit
whatever is left of the earth.

EEL

Listen to me brothers and sisters:
we have come so far together
to reach the mouth of this river.
Now it's time to turn silver and black.
You can probably feel the salt water
changing the function of your kidneys.
This is normal. If we stay together
we can describe a wide arc between
Bermuda and Puerto Rico
till we come to our birthplace —
where the currents are sluggish
and the seaweed is dense —
the perfect place to mate, spawn
and die. First we have to get there.
This sea is deep and dangerous.
Don't trust anybody — even your own
swallower and gulper cousins.
When those guys need to eat
all they do is open their mouths
and swim. This advice comes
from our ancestral memory:
trust in your sense of smell,
stay elusive and keep in line.
Okay on with the migration.
If anybody asks who we are
tell them we're snakes that swim
and we take forever to kill.

Let's go to the Sargasso.

VICEROY

The pattern on my wings is a complex
stained-glass window affair
but the message
is simple:

I am poisonous.

But I'm not. I'm aware
of the Monarch's reputation
and I trade on it. Why not?
Who wants to end up a snack
for a pernickety oriole?

It works: I'm ignored
more often than I'm devoured.

But now there are so many of me
the Monarch is sometimes mistaken
for her tasty impersonator
and is eaten.

I say to myself:
what's another sick predator?

Then
I cross the sunlit clearing
between one milkweed and another,
as slowly as I dare
wondering which of my reputations
has gone before me.

LIZARD

Slim young reptile. Prominent spines. Serrated teeth. Zygodactylous feet. Strongly recurved claws. Fully retractable tongue. Forked copulatory organs on either side of autonomous, prehensile tail. Fully adapted to life on land. Able to change colour. Luminous in caves. Capable of gliding. Interested in flies, camouflage and staying very still for long periods of the day. **WLTM** slim young reptile. Must have external ear openings, movable eyelids and limbs suited to rapid locomotion. (No snakes please.) Must be capable of internal fertilisation, producing hard-shelled eggs. To bring external heat into my three-chambered heart. For displays mating dances and mutual adherence in ambient temperatures. Poss. propagation of species.

TORTOISE

I was born prehistoric.
I know the slow
agony of mating.

The ritual spawning.
The laborious burial
of my vulnerable eggs.

Don't talk to me
about a life
of quiet desperation.

I am wise to you
in your bungalow
with your lawnmower.

You are not so unlike
a meat pie with eyes,
a helmet with legs.

You like to stay in.
How you drool to be
eligible for a pension.

You like to feed me, eh?
Watch my rude jaws murder
the peach you didn't dare eat.

BUZZARD

I'm a big bad bastard.
I've done too much solitary.
Watch this. I'll empty this tree
just by clearing my throat.
If anything runs or crawls
I'll claim it in my claw.
I'll tell you something else:
My ancestors were hawks
and vultures. I'm a serial killer.
But nowadays I've got you
to do the business for me.
In your flash steel feathers —
you're fast, I'll say that for you.
You'd make a good buzzard.
Seriously: you could be me.
I enjoy an uncooked breakfast.
Raw liver. Fresh intestines.
Specially when it's killed for me.

SEAGULL

We are the dawn marauders.
We prey on pizza. We kill kebabs.
We mug thrushes for bread crusts
with a snap of our big bent beaks.
We drum the worms from the ground
with the stamp of our wide webbed feet.
We spread out, cover the area —
like cops looking for the body
of a murdered fish-supper.
Here we go with our hooligan yells
loud with gluttony, sharp with starvation.
Here we go bungee-jumping on the wind,
charging from the cold sea of our birth.
This is invasion. This is occupation.
Our flags are black, white and grey.
Our wing-stripes are our rank.
No sun can match the brazen
colour of our mad yellow eyes.

We are the seagulls.
We are the people.

THE SAVAGE OBJECT

OBJECT

What gestures to my thirsty eye
in the quenching green
of a blade of grass?

Not art
— unless you mean what green means
when it is a blade of grass.

What do accent and emphasis insist
in the rhythms of speech
to my ravenous ear?

Not music
— unless you mean the chords
and cadence of our daily talk.

In these colours and inflections
we are offered the savage object
of the senses:

what we are given;
what we have forgotten;
what longs to find a voice.

TURNIP

The prize turnip is one of the few
to have made a name for itself
in the modern world.

The prize turnip has been criticised
by other turnips — for being a prize
and for being a turnip.

Some turnips say: 'What does it
think it is? It's just a turnip
like the rest of us.'

Other turnips argue: 'This is the point.
Why should an ordinary turnip not
be raised to prize status?'

Meanwhile the Turnip Liberation Front
has issued a statement, deploring
the exploitation of turnips.

The prize turnip does its best
to ignore the controversy.
It concentrates on being a turnip.

It dreams of being wrenched at dawn
from the hard, dark ground to be
eaten raw by hungry boys.

JAR

You have served to carry our milk
our provisions our necessary items.
Broken necklaces. Rainwater. Barley.
Ashes of our dead, for example.

You were good enough to hold
the flowers for the still life.
Even when they wilted to their image
you refrained from comment.

When you glimpsed your immortality
— before it was turned to the wall —
your lip did not tremble. You waited
to be emptied, to be filled.

Forgive us jar we were blind
to your virtues: solidity; emptiness.
Maybe it was in your interests
that we saw only your purpose.

From the childhood of artefacts
you come to me intact
with your chipped rim your mended crack —
open-mouthed in a mute plea.

Let me place my hand
on your rounded shoulder.
Set my ear to your chasm to hear
the long, boring story of the abyss.

Let me fill you
with more than my voice.
Dumb clay drum dumb clay drum —
I proclaim your worth.

And when the inevitable happens and
a rebellious elbow, a recalcitrant wrist
coups you from your ledge of being
somersaulting you into becoming —

I promise you I will try —
with all the animated antics
of my human distress —
to catch you before you smash.

KITE

So what if I'm fragile —
I continually risk my neck
just to stay where I'm not.

My life is brief, a loop-the-loop,
a figure-eight, bound to end
in a crashed catastrophe.

But my life has a purpose.
Why else does my colour's quick
tug so intently at your eye?

To gather the open sky
into your mind's shuttered room —
unravelling my rippling arrow.

I point at nothing but the vast
openness inside you. I am
a pennant of your desire.

I say play with me, play me.
I say hold me, let me go.
Hold me —

DUMPLING

Make way for the dumpling, the hero
of a Scottish kitchen's history at last.
Let us celebrate the hero dumpling,
rolled through two world wars to feed us.
Mummified in muslins, hung in clooties,
boiled for years in brilloed jeely-pans
and swathed in a fat ghost of steam.
Sedater of the nation, the dumpling
has weighed upon the bellies of kings
and beggars alike — and will again.
Rich with the sweet, ancient raisins
of our great-great-grannies' eyes.
Studded with our great-great grandads'
hard brass threepenny-bit teeth.
Here he comes, here comes the hero:
this colossal arse of a pudding
like a monster's benappied bairn.
Solid as a medicine ball, but riddled
with everyday riches: the fat
of an ox's kidneys, this poulticed
bomb of spice and suet and sweat
will keep for weeks, months, years —
it will last a lifetime of thrift,
wrapped in greaseproof, lardered,
taken out to be sliced and fried.
Here is the hero dumpling at last:
so slap the hero, slap him hard
give the hero's arse a good, hard slap.

SPOT

Then you see it: a spot, but not of rain —
a stain, but not of paint, red but not red —
darker, and again: a spot, it's bigger
than the first, it's darker — another then

another and again: a spot, a spot.
And you know with sickened recognition:
it is what it is, not what it isn't.
It will lead you to the scene of the crime.

But what if it leads you, like history
to the present, and to the crime itself —
to the bottle that's breaking, not broken?

And there is suddenly the choice of three
roles of victim, perpetrator, witness —
and which should you be and which will you be?

FLOOR

My mother liked to see
a clean, scrubbed floor.
She scoured it over and over
and dreamed of her Ideal Home:
'The kitchen is literally out of this world.
Beautiful units, freezer, rotisserie.
In the lounge, deep-pile, wall-to-wall . . . '
They were like Plato's forms,
my mother's dreams. I saw the effects:
glass swans in a mirrored alcove;
a sort of a peach-coloured settee.
I see her in her nylon housecoat,
the rolled-up hanky from her sleeve
dabbing the tears from her eyes.
She's having a good cry to heaven
before making a start on the stairs.
I inherit her dog-eared diploma
from the Institute of House Workers.
A twin-tub to be emptied pail by pail.
The way I hold my cigarette.
That sort of peach-coloured settee.
And a clean, scrubbed floor
I'll scrawl my dirty footprints over.

SETTEE

I come from the Furniture Mother
but you'll find no comfort in me.
I'm just the settee.

Even if you live with someone
you love, you'll end up alone,
not sleeping on me.

Let me spread my woodworm,
that's better. It's good to feel
I'm still part of things.

On special occasions I'll dress
in ridiculous antimacassars
to embarrass you.

If you ever get desperate enough
to search my innards for coins
you'll find razorblades.

When you can stand me no longer
you'll pay someone to come
and take me away.

COAL

In the blunted night of the coal shed,
without a torch, my fingers dig
among the coal for the coal.
Hear it scutter into the bucket.

Something else is gathered, uttered
from a darker place where memory digs
and throws its coal into a bucket —
as if a ghost stuttered, spoke:

My father clears his throat, curses
the government: 'Thirty years in Rosewell,
in Bilston Glen, in Monktonhall —
and what is there to show for it?'

And what is there to show for it?
Flattened sites, non-places, absences
surrounded by meaningless villages.
The bars look like air-raid shelters.

'If the shops need iron grilles here,
they'll need them everywhere.
Like the miners of Monktonhall
we'll all know what siege means.'

I stumble from the dark into the dark
of that night into this, to light a fire,
to watch the flames rise and flare
into eloquent tongues.

RAT

My hand discovers you. A scrap
of doormat with claws, scrubbingbrush
with teeth. Among leaves, old sacks
in the world's most unlit outhouse.

I'm a bellows that sucks the air
as the breath rushes into me
like a hunted thing — scared
of you, and of what you are not.

Hardened to the brittle, the literal
emblem of yourself. That pebble
embedded in your side is more
alive in its cool, smooth silence.

With a stick, I pick you up
by a tail as stiff as a coat hook.

Did death catch you on the hop
old enemy — as it catches those
who make a habit of survival?

I won't pick up that, I think.

Then your eyeless eye's full stop
stops me, mid-life, mid-thought,
with the riddle of your dry reminder.

I shut my eyes as I throw you
as far as I can throw your image
out of my mind's out-of-sight.

One morning I'll find you there
grinning at me from the future
of your delicate skeleton.

STONE

Of all the stones I threw as a boy
I remember only one:

unlike stones I flicked and skipped
to interrupt flat water;

bullet-stones to detonate bottles,
ding tin cans from high fences;

unlike stones thrown at headstones,
to exorcise the dead;

unlike stones thrown out of boredom
at dogs cats fish birds rats

(just to keep them on their toes)
this particular stone was thrown

— so all my sins confess themselves
at last — at a girl. And when

I watched it swoop from the air,
I shut my eyes tight — aware

that I'd get what I deserved
and more. I was guilty. Yet

in that moment I learned to care
for another, for her suffering.

So love's aim was as true
as mine. And all its longing

came down on me —
came down on me and cut me through.

BALL

The brown leather teamball
with the bootlaced mouth —
when it burst open in mid-air
the bladder's teat sprang out
and we headered a rubber udder.
It was as if all our mothers
had invaded the football pitch:
the porridge our studs made
in the goalmouth's mud
was part of a knitted balaclava
that surrounded every orifice.
That soup heavy with barley
left in the bottom of the bowl
made our hunger quicken
for the smell of slide-tackled earth,
pungent with victory or defeat.
When it was almost too dark
to see the ball, our names
came to claim us across the park
like those ghostly, neglected kids
who always turned up at the end
— wanting to know the score,
asking if there were any games.

OBJET PERDU

Pile in with all the others.
The shovel with the snarled lip.
The sieve with the hole in it.
This scissor who lost his sister.

Everyone is welcome here.
We have all outlived our duties.
We are destined for higher things.
We just have to wait to be chosen.

Think of the wine-bottle candlestick.
Think of the long-playing flowerpot.
The bull with the handlebar horns.
The urinal, signed 'R Mutt'.

Think of a crushed automobile
in the Gallery of Modern Art.
As a car, it covered Connecticut.
As Art, it covered the world.

Your turn will come, believe me.
What were you for — no idea?
So what's your handle? Okay,
Beauty — get in line behind Truth.

OTHER LIFE

OTHER LIFE

I lie in the darkness and listen
to some threadbare life in our room,

some fretful other life in our room
— it isn't me it isn't you —

at times like a breathless trust
or the spatter of a hesitant rain;

caresses of feverish shadows;
asthma of a dying candle

— it isn't you it isn't me —
can't you hear it there it is again:

a sparse stirring of the wind
in the branches of a leafless tree.

You say: It's just
the jenny-long-legs, that's all.

I know. Though even that
sounds more description than name.

In my cupped hand it is
some scarce yearning grown restless:

a desire searching for a gesture;
a love looking for its word.

ORDINARY WORDS

Time hurries between us,
like garrulous water.

There's a metaphor here
with a gossiping stream
full of blethering pebbles
and the rumour of fish.

But that runs between us too —
you on your bank, me on mine.

I could shout the inanities of love
and be drowned out by the roar
of the rapids of my desire,
but then you'd mouth back, 'What?'

Instead, I lean forward to ask:
'D'you want a drink, love?'

Time hurries between us
and I bridge it with the ordinary
words like 'want' and 'drink'
— and that rickety old word 'love'.

SICK KID

A father's hand comes to rest
on his baby's incubator.
I read to you from a book
which belongs to no one.

Trapped in the story we are in
we must listen to the others:
the story of a cow who can't moo
and a clock that goes tock-tick.

The boy with the fractured skull
and a jealous stepfather.
Or the one about the girl
who is growing another skin.

That gargantuan teddy bear
manacled to the radiator
— a hostage of childhood
grown into a forlorn monster —

makes a tiny adult of me
afraid of your vast innocence.
It is you must reassure me
as I hush you to sleep.

Outside the wind roams the night
like a giant fleeing ridicule.
Maybe another troubled father
is fretful for his sick kid, the earth.

NURSERY SCHOOL

The hammer, the saw and the pliers
cling to their painted silhouettes —
objects so fundamental
they grow permanent shadows.

On folded, unfolded pages
stapled to the wall, a swarm
of coloured symmetries surround
one dark, bivalve mollusc.

In its private sahara, a stick
impersonates a stick-insect.
A budgie head-butts its clone
in the other cage in its mirror.

The harassed giant blunders
into the play house — his daughter
waits for him with watchful eyes
and a thimble full of water.

ANGEL

The three wise men are cardboard
toilet-roll tubes with moustaches.
A Barbie-doll veiled in Andrex
stands in for the Virgin Mary.

A mauled doll from another mother,
passed down through every birth
to be loved to death, is cast
as the doomed and lovely Christ.

I receive a message from a minister
exhorting me to rediscover
the church I have neglected,
as if I were its unholy father.

So I rediscover the streets.
In the window of the fruit shop
someone has thoughtfully placed
a solitary lemon balloon.

Under the star of Tollcross,
made of coloured light bulbs,
two homeless men share a bottle,
excuse themselves, demand change.

Barclay Church eyebrows an arch
and looks down its long, gothic nose
at the Tollcross Video Library
and Mohammed's 'Global Vegetables'.

Christmas has trimmed the windows
inside the Auld Toll Bar
with an aerosol scrawl
of italicised snow.

The fallen angel stands at the bar,
a pre-Christian carving of himself.
He sees me and says, 'Poison.
I'll leave the measure up to you.'

IT

Mohammed's lovely daughter
who has been lately married

sweeps over the road
in her robes of blue and silver —

like the earth, wrapped around
by the sea and the sky.

The woman from number five
with dead hair, squint specs

— a skeleton in a raincoat,
an absence with an opinion —

says, 'There's anither yin
that thinks she's It.'

BUDDHA

I met the Buddha in Edinburgh:
hunkered in a doorway in the West Bow,
a can of Carlsberg in his hand.

Around him shops, cops and dogs
were doing their miserable business.
He was doing his:

with a hand as black as a tenement
he wiped his oracular mouth,
growled his simple teachings:

Fuck-all point. Fuck-all point.
Lost the lot. Lost the lot.
Guid riddance. Guid riddance.

And he watched me, the nothing I was
as I passed. He watches me still
crouched in a doorway in my mind

in that inelegant, Scottish half-lotus,
the void of the afternoon
in the void of his eyes.

VISITING SPEAKER

Once there was a visiting speaker
who didn't speak.
He addressed no one:
no one came.

His talk did not take place
in a place called Aberdeen.

Afterwards he drank a lot
but couldn't get drunk
and stayed at a guest house
where he was the only guest.

When he went home, his wife
found him strangely changed.
It was as if she embraced
an absence.

When she asked what the matter was
he said: 'I take it you refer
to the Manichaean doctrine
of inherent evil in matter?'

More irritating still was the way
he kept glancing at his watch,
asking for a glass of water
and thanking her for coming.

ISLAND GIRL

Her voice has a musical precision
even as she tells me
of the storm at sea
of the fishermen drowned.

The haphazard silhouette
of her village with its tiny harbour
ugly kirk and awry graveyard
is mirrored in her calm green eye.

And the cruel beauty of the sea.
And the cruel beauty of the sky.
Look closer: all her people
are being born and dying there.

So much is evolving in her eye
to paint it I'd need a canvas
the length and breadth of Lewis —
a brush as fine as her eyelash.

APHRODITE

To what summer's day shall I compare
the private jacuzzis of your eyes?
You're pure manicure. You're slow-motion hair.
You're a stocking's silk complexion of sighs.
You're the close-up of a smile, telling lies.
Which magic, slimline girdle do you wear?
As your breasts into their *Wonderbra* rise,
I wonder, if I knew you, would I dare
take your fast-tan arm? Would I satisfy
your insatiable demands for *Milk Tray* ?
Would I splash on the *Aramis* and would I
be your bronzed, helicoptering fiancé
— one of those gods of war who never die —
or Hephaestus, with your drink on a tray?

ROY ORBISON

Anything you want —

Forever old in your mourning shades
widowed hairstyle, coffin-tight suit
and a big brother's bootlace tie,
you turned Juke Box Jury into a funeral.
Your wounded tremolo made us long
for the martyrdom of 'personal tragedy'.

Anything you need —

How you pined for that Mystery Girl
who left you to burn and burn eternally.
You were not the only Only One
to blame it on your Careless Heart.
You taught us that pretty women
are not the truth, that Love Hurts.

Anything at all —

Still your grieving falsetto keens to us
from its scratchy sixties heaven.
Missing You, it says. Only the Lonely,
bereaved of youth, never die:
stuck in our groove, In the Real World,
we go on and on Roy Orbisoning.

You got it.

SURASUNDARI

I've danced from Khajuraho
over oceans and centuries
via Byzantium and Dubai
to this museum in Edinburgh

— and I'm dancing still.

My last engagement was a temple
but I don't mind where I'm on —
I can do what I'm good at
in a fragment of stone

— dancing. Watch me dancing.

You don't have to put my name
in the dictionary of mythology.
I was always the supporting act
in the drama of the deities

— I was just a dancer, dancing.

Again I entrance
your steps to a stop.
I invite your casual glance
to follow the pulse of my form

— watch the dancer, dancing.

See the inflection of the wrist
in my missing arm — there is
the delicate, questioning poise
of the elephant's trunk

— he needs no arms for dancing.

The beads that emboss the swell
of my voluptuous hips —
hear me shake them, make them hiss
the insinuations of the snake

— he needs no legs for dancing.

My skin is also the snake's.
I've shed it over and over
to bare the truth — that music
can animate a stone

— and make it dance, like this.

RECLINING NUDE

On a blood-red chaise-longue,
fanning her drooping eyelids
with the heat of her hot coal mouth,
she is still reclining and reclining
into our savage history.

So, with this swooning movement,
the female presents her breasts
and her glowing abdomen
whose adhesive tendrons
guide the sperm to her eggs.

Armies queue up to rape her.
Painters queue up to paint her.
Collectors queue up to collect her.
Businessmen queue up to sell
shares in her reclining hospitality.

Then the stretched bow of her back
shoots the arrow of her pubic hair
and the reclining nude stands up,
tells them their century is over
and holds a press conference.

SWAN

Aye, Ah feed her.
They need tae eat.
Same as you and me.
Ah gie her a bit o my piece.
Unless she's no there.
Or unless Ah'm no.
Like at the week-end.
In the Leisure Centre
when Ah'm rackin up
Ah think aboot her. Ah
wonder if she's hungry.
Then Ah feel hungry.
Ah say tae ma mate:
D'ye fancy a kebab?
She's no fussy either.
Eats anythin Ah throw her.
Some neck on her, eh?
Like the handle on a cup.

Watch this, she'll come to me.

THE RAT CATCHER

1

Rats, is it? Dinnae tell me about rats.
Ah've been catchin the buggers aw ma life.
An killin them — by the score. Still as rife
as ever. What's the point, ye say? That's

what Ah say tae. If there's work Ah'll take it.
What's the matter, boss? Have ye never seen
a man like me, wi different-coloured een?
D'ye no like ma reversible jaiket?

Dinnae talk tae me about Rentokil.
Ah can smell a rat withoot they newfangled
rodent-sensors. Me an my wee pal Bill

— he's ma ferret — smell them out onywhaur.
Even in this — *Yaughpteow!* — oak-panelled,
toon-cooncil suite in the private sector.

2

Mind you — *Grimhauch!* — Ah'm no sayin that
Ah can provide a fool-proof guarantee
Of a rodent-free premises. Ye see,
cooncils come and go, but there'll ay be rats.

Wait'll Ah shift this filin cabinet.
This job's no — *Achyub-b-ba* ...! — as straightforward
as ye might think, even though it's no hard
tae track them by their droppins tae the nest.

But there's rats and rats. What d'ye think of thon
lang-nebbed, big-eared bastard in the Depart
-ment of Leisure and Recreation?

Ken whae Ah mean? Aye, a lad o parts.
A right sleekit bugger. Disnae let on
he sees ye. Aye, him in charge of the Arts.

3

Ah'll need tae disconnect yer computer
for a minute. Sorry tae interrupt
yer meetin. Ah'm sure yous are no as corrupt
as it says in the paper. But Ah've heard

there's rats in high places — ken whae Ah mean?
Thon Director of Housing, what's-his-name,
Aye, him. Ye should see the hoose he lives in.
An yet there's folk are homeless. It's obscene.

Aye Ah'll droon them aw doon at the river.
They're callin them the doomed generation.
They must be somebody's sons an daughters.

They judges in their robes trimmed wi ermine.
They'd mibbe recognise the problem
if they classed men as men, no as vermin.

4

Ye've got tae grip him tight aroond the neck.
Gie the bugger hauf a chance — he'll bite ye.
He's feart — *grimhauch!* He kens he's gonnae dee.
If ye swing him by the tail, it'll breck

like a twenty-pee stick of liquorice.
Ah've battered their heids on the windaesill.
Ah've drooned them in their cages. Aye but still
there's mair where they came frae. When Ah finish

ma job, Ah've got tae start aw owre again.
Suits me. Ah dinnae want tae make masel
redundant, like. Ah'm a survivor, ken?

Like yer average rat. Ye don't need tae tell
him the world doesnae owe him a livin.
He's a family man. He kens it fine well.

5

Any kiddies, boss? What's that — just the one?
Every bairn is a blessin and a curse.
Ah say tae ma youngest: ye could dae worse
than a career in extermination.

Doesnae listen to me though. Likes to stand
on his ain two feet. Aw aye? That's a shame.
Naebody tellt me your wee boy was lame.
Mine's musical — wants to be in a band

— no a Rodent Control Operator.
Sounds grand, eh? That's ma job description noo.
What's yours? Socialism withoot clause four?

Ah smell a rat. Least Ah'm no on the burroo.
At the end of the day Ah'm just a man
whae needs tae make a livin, same as you.

RECRUIT

Don't look so come on now don't
look so sincere you are too young
for such a frown. You have a girl?
A pity. Maybe you will find a girl
in your services for us, although
as you know we are not a dating agency.
Leave that unwieldy ideal by the door.
What is it? A shapely idea, a painted lie.
In any case you won't need it here.
You were chosen because of your truck.
We want you to deliver some explosives
to the fruit market. A man called Harry
will be expecting you. He has a stall.
He owes us a favour more than one.
Harry will relieve you of your apples.
I think it will be apples or potatoes.
So when you are stopped at the border
you will show them your papers as usual.
Of course, the truck will be searched.
Here is a picture of one of the guards —
look at him carefully, remember him.
He will do the search, while the other
checks your papers. Well that's it
I'm sure everything will go smoothly.
The man called Harry has a daughter
she is young like you, better looking.
Maybe you will meet her, fall in love.
The only other thing is the apples

or potatoes as the case may be.
Make sure the man called Harry
gives you a decent price for them.
As I said he owes us a favour.
We're not running a charity here.
Go now. Drive carefully. Go.

THOUSAND

You have read the paper too you know
the story of the thousand forced to flee
their disputed region though no doubt
the thousand called it something else
such as home for example here
no it did not say what forced them
nor whether they were forced to go
together towards the same unknown
or to scatter as insects scatter
when their stone is lifted I imagine
they had time to round up the kids
take their old if not infirm maybe
a cherished horse a particular goat
the dogs would no doubt follow
after all they were the thousand
and would pack what food they had
a bag of apples tipped from a bowl
a live chicken maybe a t.v. dinner
what about the t.v. what about the radio
leave them what have they done for us
take that amulet this certificate
those plates cups spoons a good knife
whatever can be crammed into the pram
on the roof rack in the wheelbarrow
it won't be much it won't be much
our time is short our warning brief
we ourselves don't know where to go
and the question how to get there

will have to be answered on the way
we must flee and keep on fleeing
until the day you open your doors
and find us standing there and say
you must be the thousand come in
we have read about you take a seat
stay here make yourselves at home
until you get your disputed region back
that doesn't happen though does it
we have read the paper too we know

MERCY

I said to him:
have you come to slaughter us?

Is that why you have come?
Shut up, he said.

As soon as he said it I heard
the knife coming out.

He stabbed me here
and here and here and here —

twenty-nine times he stabbed me.
He did this the way you mix cement.

He threw me down among my blood.
He said:

I've slaughtered so many today,
but I've come across no one like this.

Someone said:
leave her, she is finished.

Go and cut the children's throats
so that they won't suffer.

So he cut the children's throats
so that they wouldn't suffer.

BODY PARTS

WE

are tired of appearing as diagrams
in medical encyclopaedias
and close-ups in t.v. ads
for Anadin and Oil of Ulay.
We can't go on eviscerating
for the camera in *Casualty*.
We have lost the desire to star
in hard-core XXXX videos
available by mail-order only.
Or to be posted in litter-bins —
botched parcels to be sorted
into freezer-drawers in a morgue.
Or to lurk in buckets like
stunned eels awaiting deliverance.
At one time — loyal employees
of an old-fashioned firm —
we refused to be transplanted.
We were imperfect but faithful.
Now we have developed the ability
to move from one host to another
by helicopter. Packaged in ice,
marked 'URGENT — CHICAGO',
we are ready for reincarnation.

We know the art market.
We are willing to cross species.
We have come to terms with fame.
We want change. We demand evolution.

SCAPULA

When I move my arm, I'm reminded
by a scything pain
that death the reaper is not just
an illustrative Mediaeval woodcut.

Behind my back, my doctor stoops
to confide in my tendons.

'Aha, scapula,' he says
as if to soothe it with the sound
of its Latin name.

To me, off-hand, he enquires:
'Does it hurt when you shrug?'
My answer's a shrug, and it does.

He chuckles diagnostically,
shakes his head and consoles:
'Poor large, flat, triangular bone.'

He admonishes me: 'You're a writer, eh?
An unhealthy profession.

All those drinks with publishers, agents
of death. No doubt you smoke
while you write and while you don't,
while you wait for your great inspiration.

Don't talk to me about Balzac.
All those cups of strong black coffee,
all that burning the midnight oil —
I know what you chaps get up to.

Contemplating the eternal verities
is very bad news for the scapula.
Give up literature, my friend —
your shoulder blade will thank you for it.'

TONGUE

You catch my eye as I'm shaving
with a quick, sidelong lick —
old friend we are both grown older
and shudder at the sight of each other.

You amorous eel you.
You visceral lizard.
So you represent the innards.
So you are sent with a petition:

The living conditions of the liver . . .
The diligence of the duodenum . . .
The drainage of the lymph glands . . .
The work-rate of the testes . . .

Yes, yes — thank you, tongue.
Your loyalty will be rewarded.
Tell them it has been noted.
Tell them I am in a meeting.

Now what is it you are after —
some slippery thing? A slice of melon?
A new texture? What do you want —
another tongue to love, or what?

EYELIDS

As a boy I had a friend
who could turn his inside-out.

This feat he performed
with great economy
when his audience had assembled:
the one and then the other.

He stood there: arms akimbo,
eyes hooded in flanges of blood,
a helpless fiend. The vulnerable
demon of Viewbank Road.

When we lit fires
and discussed the future,
he contorted his genitals
to make them impersonate a girl's.

His *tour de force*
was to make his impudent prick
stand to attention and weep
hot, thick tears of remorse.

It deserved applause, but
we sat in stunned wonder,
watching his delicate eyelids
close in the soft firelight.

HAND

After the floggings the mutilations.
After the mutilations the executions.
In the square the thief waits in line
and he whispers to his hand:

'Forgive me hand I am sorry
for teaching you how to steal.
I misled you my faithful hand.
It was a partnership of a kind.

I will miss you my clever hand.
You will be better without me.
You will just be a hand any hand.
Your duties to me are finished.

The other is no good as you know.
Begging will be more its line.
You were always the talented one.
You are not to blame.

We should not have taken
that star fruit that star fruit
was too colourful and shapely.
What did we want with a star fruit?'

From the parchment is read out
the thief's name, his crime.
People yawn, scratch themselves
and examine their hands.

FEET

I knew this something like this
had to happen there was no choice
to defend our village our homes
then there was nothing to defend
if there was a choice I made it
long ago I made it with my feet
for survival my family my people
my feet were not to blame for this
they were ordinary feet I ignored
my feet all my life they were just
my obedient feet my precious feet
they took me from the kitchen
to the bathroom from the village
to the mountain they did not know
any better than to run from the enemy
they were taking me to the border
when it happened why am I
being photographed like this
for a newspaper I won't read
apparently I have no choice
I know what the caption will say
a fugitive is carried to the border
having stepped on a land mine
so much for my caption it is true
I am being carried from now on
I will have to be carried because

I have lost my feet I have no feet

MOUTH

As you cram your mouth
with some very earthly delights,
your golden hair shines, like
plucked harp-strings in the light.

That is called a simile.

In your skin's glow is
the apparition of fruit.
Your hesitant confidences are
the cries of extinct birds.

A couple of metaphors.

Angel, come and sit on my knee
hear your father's bitter words
as he savours your sweetness.
Repeat after me: never

accept similes or metaphors
from the mouths of strangers.

SMALL INTESTINE

I don't know much about my duodenum:
only that it is part of my small intestine
between my stomach and my jejunum,
and that its name means the intestine
of twelve fingers' length — twelve, not ten,
as if the duodenum is unwilling
to be gauged by human hands.

All I know of my jejunum is that
it is part of my small intestine
between my duodenum and my ileum
and that its name means empty —
from the belief that it is empty after death.
I would like to think that my jejunum
will not disgrace itself
and after death will maintain
an emptiness worthy of its name.

On the subject of my ileum I know
next to nothing, but that it is
the part of my small intestine
between my jejunum and my caecum
and that insects have one too.
Tunnel from jejunum to caecum,
bridge between insect and man.
If only every part of me
showed such versatility.

My caecum, as you may have guessed,
is something of a mystery to me:
all I know is that this poor, blind pouch
marks the start of my large intestine
and is, strictly speaking,
outwith the scope of this poem.

Small intestine with your four strange gods
— duodenum, jejunum, ileum, caecum.

Forgive me.

HEAD

I submit that the accused — this
abbatoir-butcher-turned-sculptor
so favoured by the Prince of Wales —
bought the said anatomical specimen
— which he knew to be stolen —
from his co-accused — the former
Royal College of Surgeons technician.
He then took the said head
to his family seat in Kent
and covered it — by what process
I know not — in silver. And exhibited it,
ladies and gentlemen of the jury,
at the Islington Arts Fair. I refer you
to page one of the catalogue marked 'A'.
I think you will agree that this 'Head'
is lifelike. Very. It has been admired
by His Royal Highness personally.

Perhaps neither he nor the accused
were troubled by the fact that
a section of the brain
is missing.

HEAD 2

We come as the deputation
for the campaign to free Yagan.
The head of Yagan is in Liverpool.
The body of Yagan in Australia.

The spirit of Yagan will be free
when the head of Yagan
is reunited, as it will be,
with the body of Yagan.

The head of Yagan is no trophy
though Yagan is a warrior.
The head of Yagan no exhibit
though Yagan is a leader.

The body of Yagan waits for
the head of Yagan to come home.
No one will receive Yagan
till the spirit of Yagan is free.

We the undersigned
demand the head of Yagan.
Tell the experts to look for
the bullet-hole in the skull.

DONOR

I signed a form giving my consent.
So technically I am the donor.

The papers have had a field day.
The Sun called me Son of Frankenstein.
The Independent freaked me in another way
with its 'haunting ethical questions'.

The question that haunted me
was this: if I survive — who will I be?
I have, and I'm still who I am, but
it's as if a stranger has become me.

Sometimes when I touch myself
I want to tell him I'm sorry.
When he goes to the bathroom
I want to look the other way.

I tell myself: the donor
was the brain-dead head
whose body I have inherited.
Maybe one day we'll be intimate.

Something his wife said scared me.
She said: 'In you, my John lives on.'
We smiled for the cameras
both afraid of rejection.

My lawyers have advised me
that she does have a case.

SKULL

The X-ray of my daughter's skull is vast.
This moth with its dark wings of smoke
is a map of the undiscovered world.
Continents part, seas come together
and dark lands bear no legend.

I speak to her one to one —
though our scales are different.
The giant I am in her land
lumbers in murmured words
that boom in her head like bombs.

Then I'm Gullivered, tethered
by a smile from her Lilliputian lips —
as she snatches the acetate shadow
of her precious skull from my hands
and claims it as her own.

COCK

I went into work one morning
and it was sitting in my in-tray.
Everyone oohd and aahd and
tried to guess whose it was.

I reported it to my boss.
I said I felt sorry for a man
who could photocopy that
and expect it to be a turn-on.

He took me out for dinner
and confessed that it was his.
He tried it on, but the thought
of his A4 monster put me off.

He promoted me in due course.
When I moved to Single Design
and his assets were sequestered,
I showed it to the boys in printing.

It was Steve, the cute one, who said
that he'd used the enlarger.
So often in this business I find
the idea of size does matter.

EAR

In the night my wanton ear
grows invisible tendrils of hearing.
No doubt if it were a hand
it would reach out for something:

the footfall of a lover returning;
a sigh without resignation;
the whispered insinuation
of your dress on your skin.

My adulterous ear, it savours
their textures and their tints
until, grown corrupt with longing
it steals away from me in sleep.

It lets itself out of the house,
listens down along the street,
receives the whisper of a mist.
My ear in its yearning reaches out

for the distant shout of a star
as it burns and burns with desire,
for the white noise of the universe
breathing in another's ear.

NODE

A part of me is still hers, I wrote,
then wondered — which part?

The rogue, inchlong hair
sprouting from my left eyebrow
you teased between your fingertips?

The nipple that flinched
from your thrilling fingernail
and its scything caress?

The gully in my groin
where your travelling tongue
paused to probe a lymph node?

But I didn't know I had
any of those parts of me
until you found them out.

I write:
A part of her is still mine . . .

SKIN

In the newspaper I read about
a man impaled on a stick
who was skinned alive
and left to die.

My skin does not forget
the agonies of its brother skin.
Nor will it be consoled by water.
It dreams of knives.

It sweats salt tears.
Itches with vicarious horror.
My skin's imagination is
a rash of nightmarish inflictions.

I try to placate it with the notion
that this won't happen to us,
hush it with the promise of caresses
from the skin of another.

My skin won't have any of it.
It whispers to me:
this is where you and I
part company. Goodbye.

THIGH

'It's this ache in my temple, Doctor.
My heart beats too loud, too fast.
My shoulder problem is back
and I can't sleep at night.
I think I'm going to die.'

He clears the sarcasm from his throat
to enquire: 'Nothing else?'

'Well, yes — it's probably nothing —
this rash on my thigh.'

He reserves for me
his most professional smile
and orders me to drop my pants.

'I've read your books. My diagnosis
is this: too much of you in the anti-hero;
aches, palpitations, fibrositis. Insomnia
indeed. Tell him to give up smoking,
take exercise. Tell him his hypochondria
is a tiresome affectation. As for this—'

With a fingernail he scratches
the eczema from my thigh,
stands up, tightens his tie
and licks dry lips.

'You will be pleased to know
that at last you are correct.
You are going to die.'

Brian McCabe has published two previous poetry collections: *Spring's Witch* and *One Atom to Another*; two collections of stories: *The Lipstick Circus* and *In a Dark Room with a Stranger*; and a novel, *The Other McCoy*. Four of his books have been given Scottish Arts Council Awards. He was the Scottish/Canadian Exchange Fellow in 1998–9 and has held many residencies and fellowships, most recently as novelist in residence at the University of St Andrews. He lives in Edinburgh with his family.

Praise for *One Atom to Another*

'His narrative is clean and economical, his images are bright, his cadences audible and his verse very well made.'   Douglas Dunn

'A spiky, observant writer with a lethal wit.'
                         Kate Saunders, *Scotland on Sunday*

'A Scottish writer too gifted to be shunted over to the shelf marked "regional".'
                              Maureen Freely, *Options*

'His poetry ought to be better known than it is this side of the border. He's versatile with form, trying his hand at anything from the entirely unpunctuated to the sonnet, but rarely sacrificing his subjects to formal cleverness.'   City Limits

'McCabe knows instinctively that poetry comes from the current speech of the people, and in turn, purifies and enriches it. He has the kind of imagination that can enter into any situation and any character. He has an immense span, both as satirist and celebrator. Apart from his other gifts, he is a very good craftsman.'
                      George Mackay Brown, *The Scotsman*